TEE TIME WITH DADDY
My First Nine

written by Kristin Dooley

illustrated by Daniela Sosa

FIRST EDITION

Dooley Noted Publishing, LLC
www.dooleynotedpublishing.com

ISBN-13: 978-0-692-10383-8
Library of Congress Cataloging-in-Publication Data has been applied for.

This book is dedicated to my father, Rich Cowles.

Thank you for teaching me to keep my eye on the ball,
smile and envision where I want to land.

All my love, your daughter.

Hi, my name is Lilly!
My favorite time is tea-time with my favorite friends.
We wear our white gloves with lace and pearls and sip from teacups.
I feel so grown up.

Daddy has his tee-time too.

"Daddy," I asked,
"When can I come to your
tee-time?"
"When you're older," he said,
"because of all the walking,
driving, chipping, putting and
socializing that will not
accept quitting."

Sometimes Daddy's tee-time starts at dawn and seems to last oh so long.

Today I am older so I decide to ask Daddy
if today is the day he will bring me
to his tee-time.
He reminds me of all the walking, driving,
chipping, putting and socializing that
would not accept any quitting.
"Are you sure you still want to attend?"
he asks.

"YES!"
I cheer as loudly as I can!

Daddy and I arrive to his tee-time. This is not what I had in mind. There are no pearls, no tea, and very few girls. This is different, new, and a bit scary but also very exciting. It looks like a large green park. Daddy says we are on a golf course, and I am about to play my first nine holes.

Only ladies get to play from the ladies' tees and since I always make sure
to say please, I know this will come with ease...
Daddy gives me a special golf hat, a new white glove and clubs just my size.
I also get to play so much closer to the green than Daddy.
I am sure this is a game I will love.

We start to play,
SWISH
I miss!
I swing again.
MISS!

I feel my face turn bright red.
This time I am determined to hit the ball and I do!
But it only rolls down the hill with such a long way still to go.
Daddy reminds me to rotate, not sway, and stay positive.

With a different club this time,
I walk to my ball and try again.
I miss.
I want to scream!
Tears sting my eyes.
I feel like quitting.
I want to throw my club,
but throw my hat instead!

But then I remember Daddy's words.
I walk back to my ball to try again. I take a deep breath,
look towards the waving flag, think happy thoughts and smile.
I imagine where I want my ball to land.
I write "smile" on my ball so I'll know it's mine
no matter where it falls.

Sometimes my ball falls in the sandboxes
which I think is great! I really love the sand
and have many great sandcastles I know how to make.

"Hey! Those are not sandboxes those are sand TRAPS,
we try to stay out of them," says Daddy.
"You now have to rake the mess you made!"

And then there is the lake. The lake that takes and takes.
To the right, to the left, wherever there is a lake,
my ball almost always finds The Taking Lake.

But then I think my happy thoughts. I swing, TING!!! This time I do not miss!
My ball soars straight for miles and miles. It feels so good to hit my golf ball
straight past those tricky sand traps, beyond The Taking Lake,
and up on the green closer to the pin to putt my ball in!

Tee box after tee box, hole after
hole, putt after putt, and hour after
hour, I'm having fun and
I'm getting better!

My hands ache and are sore with blisters. My feet feel as heavy as boulders and my golf bag weighs as much as an elephant! Daddy says if I can make it to the end, he has a surprise waiting for me.

What can it be?
I can't wait to find out!

Finally, we make it to the last hole. Waiting for us on the ninth green are all my favorite friends! They are dressed in their lace and pearls. Daddy and I sit and drink from tea cups with all my favorite girls. After all the walking, driving, chipping, putting, this must be the socializing part that I couldn't imagine quitting.

My favorite tea-time will always be at Daddy's tee-time.
What a special way to spend a day.

CPSIA information can be obtained
at www.ICGtesting.com
Printed in the USA
BVHW051513290419
546835BV00019B/1206/P

9 780692 103838